Diego Savani

Cinque Terre

Portovenere and Gulf of the Poets

Edizioni Giacché

The Cinque Terre

Liguria's geography

Liguria is one of Italy's twenty regions. It is to the northwest of the peninsula on the Ligurian Sea. It borders on Piedmont, Tuscany, Emilia Romagna and France. The land is prevalently mountainous: its highest peak, Monte Saccarello, reaches 2200 meters (7200 feet) above sea level. Slopes in Liguria are steep and form many valleys inland. The hills on the coast create cliffs and offer magnificent views of the sea. There are not many rivers; the longest of those that originate in Liguria is the Vara, 58 kilometers (36 miles) in length, which flows behind the Cinque Terre.

Liguria is divided into four provinces: Genoa, La Spezia, Savona and Imperia. The region's capital and most important city is Genoa; it is at the center of the region and has a population of about 580,000. The coast to the east of Genoa is known as the Liguria di Levante and it is here, on this jagged coast, that we find the Cinque Terre. The largest city in eastern Liguria is **La Spezia**, at the center of the gulf of the same name, with about 92,000 inhabitants. From here it is easy to reach the main Italian cities such as Milan (159 km)(99 miles), Pisa (83 km)(52 miles), Turin (210 km)(130 miles) and Parma (95 km)(59 miles).

The five towns

The Cinque Terre, **Riomaggiore, Manarola, Corniglia, Vernazza** and **Monterosso** are grouped into three municipalities of La Spezia province: Monterosso, Vernazza and Riomaggiore (Corniglia is part of Vernazza and Manarola of Riomaggiore). They are in the area between Punta Montenero and the Mesco promontory. Overall, they have a resident population of about five thousand, but this number increases in summer.

The land framing them is one of Italy's most beautiful, containing precious works of art, plant species, cultural, rural and seafaring traditions. For their special nature, they were declared a UNESCO **World Heritage Site** in 1997. The land is part of the **Cinque Terre National Park**, which includes a **Marine Protected Area** and a part of the hills behind the towns. In the sea are fish and marine species among the most interesting and best preserved of the Mediterranean; it is also common to catch sight of dolphins and whales.

The five towns of medieval origin remained isolated and conserved their characteristics up to the first half of the 20th century, when new access roads were opened up. Today, visitors arrive here from all over the world in search of the ancient fascination still offered by the Cinque Terre, immersed in a splendid landscape sculpted by human activities over the centuries.

Fishing and farming were the predominant activities: in the 16th century the capture of tuna at Monterosso was quite profitable and represented a third of the community's income. But what is most striking is how the people have modeled the landscape in hundreds of years, exploiting the land plot by plot to wrench from the soil produce such as grapes, lemons and olives, which have made the Cinque Terre renowned for the production of wine and oil starting from the Middle Ages.

The Second World War

During the second world conflict, Italy was under the dictatorship of Mussolini and allied

with Germany and Japan. On September 8, 1943, the government capitulated to the Allies (Great Britain, the United States and the Soviet Union) and signed an unconditional surrender. Italy was immediately occupied by the German troops. The Allies and Italian partisans fought to free the country and this came about on April 25, 1945. The upheavals caused by the war also involved the Cinque Terre, where many joined the partisan battalions.

Even now we can see the remains of the military outposts; they are mostly pillboxes and defensive structures for the sighting of aircraft and ships. Those we find at Monterosso are interesting: they are on the rocks below the ancient Aurora tower and the Corone promontory located at the beginning of the trail to Vernazza. On the Punta del Mesco, still at Monterosso, we can see the remains of an Italian Navy beacon that you can visit along the trail to Levanto.

A plaque in Piazza Garibaldi recalls the battle that took place in the night of June 15, 1944, when the warships of the German Kriegsmarine were attacked in front of Monterosso by three American torpedo boats under the command of the British Coastal Forces. The town's fishermen who witnessed the battle saved the survivors in their rowboats.

Life in the Cinque Terre

The inhabitants of the Cinque Terre lead a quiet life in contact with nature, but complicated by certain limits. Building, for example, is rigidly regulated by laws that try to protect the land. The stairways leading up to the typical *case torri* ("tower houses") that characterize the towns are steep and narrow and the apartments consist for the most part of four or five small rooms. They are old buildings in a precious environment enjoying worldwide renown and so their prices tend to be prohibitive. This is why it is not easy to find hotels or resorts except in Monterosso, where the lay of the land makes the construction of larger buildings possible. But it is easy to find bed & breakfast lodgings or rooms for rent offered by families.

Residents are forced to travel by train or car to their jobs in the cities; many commuters reach La Spezia or Genoa every day.

Because of the poor road network, goods are carried mostly by sea or train, which is the best means of transportation. If you wonder how to reach the farm houses scattered on the hills, the only way is to go on foot, climbing up steep stairways.

The buses can reach Riomaggiore and Manarola by using the coastal road, a beautiful panoramic route connecting the two towns to La Spezia.

As concerns **health**, there are pharmacies in each town and, except in emergencies, doctors visit their patients on a weekly basis.

Landscapes and typical products

The inhabitants have succeeded in exploiting the hillsides by terracing the land with dry-stone walls one above the other that support the so-called *piane* or *cian*. Near the coast these plots are narrow and usually have just one row of vines. The stones used are local sandstone, worked and put in place using centuries-old techniques.

The Cinque Terre are twinned with the **Chinese Wall**; it has been calculated that over the centuries 6729 km (4181 miles) of *muretti* have been built. Placed one after the other, they would be almost as long as the famous wall in China, which is some 7000 km (4350 miles) in length. The twinning took place in Beijing in 2006. It provides for cultural exchanges and tourism respecting the environmental sustainability of the two world heritage sites.

The dry walls are the main characteristic of the land. They have shaped it and modified its landscapes, but they require constant maintenance. Today however, only a fourth of the old terraced plots have been conserved and are cultivated. Working this land calls for sacrifice and constant commitment. The young people who choose to do this make a life choice, and they are few. A serious threat is also represented by building speculation which risks jeopardizing a naturally fragile coastal area and compromising a centuries-old equilibrium between humans and nature.

The extraordinary properties of Cinque Terre wines have been known since the Middle Ages, when they were exported all over Europe. In the 1920s and 30s the vines were destroyed by a parasite (the vine louse) and this entailed the hard task of grafting a resistant species onto the native rootstock. Today the grapes grown are **Bosco, Albarola and Vermentino,** which produce mostly a designation of origin (DOC) white wine. But the most precious traditional wine of the Cinque Terre is *Sciacchetrà*, a fine dessert wine. The harvest is in September and the bunches of grapes are hung in the cellars to dry for forty days, after which they are pressed and the result is a wine with the warm, intense color of the sun.

Another product is **olive oil**, especially in the area of Corniglia, Vernazza and on the hills of Volastra and Monterosso, produced from trees that are now hundreds of years old. It is a dark green oil, as tangy and strong as the land on which the farmers harvest the olives starting from October.

Another typical product of the Monterosso area are **lemons** from which are made juices, liqueurs and cosmetics. The Monterosso bay, protected from the winds, is better than the others for citrus groves which are sensitive to the winter cold.

Cuisine

Derived from the tradition of farmers and fishermen, the typical dishes are simple, based on fish or vegetables. The **anchovies** of Monterosso are renowned; put under salt, they are the main ingredient of the *tegame*

di acciughe alla vernazzana (pan of anchovies Vernazzana style).

Typical of Liguria is **pesto**, a green sauce made with minced basil leaves, olive oil, salt, cheese and garlic. In delicatessens you can sample the *torte di riso* (rice cakes) or *torte di verdura* (vegetable tarts). Another typically Ligurian product is the *focaccia*, a soft flat bread to be found just about everywhere in the Cinque Terre: the tasty recipe calls for flour, water, salt, yeast and olive oil.

In shops selling local products you can find *testaroli* on sale: these are typical of the inland part of the Cinque Terre and are made with flour and water. They are baked in special firebrick molds called *testi*; they are boiled and then seasoned with pesto, tomato sauce or *salsa di noci* (walnut sauce), another local treat. **Seafood** in the Cinque Terre is tasty no matter how it is prepared, and this includes shellfish, octopuses and **mussels**, which in La Spezia are called *muscoli*. They are cultivated in the gulf and prepared in many different ways. In these five fishing towns you can enjoy the *capon magro*, an ancient dish with fish and vegetables. The name derives from the tradition that prohibited meat on the

days of penitence before Easter and imposed eating "magro" (lean).

In Monterosso they prepare the **torta Monterossina,** a cake with a bottom of sponge cake topped with cream, chocolate and jam.

If you visit La Spezia you will come across the **farinata**, a kind of soft flat bread made with chickpea flour, and the typical **mes-ciüa** legume soup.

The climate

In the Cinque Terre the temperature is mild throughout the year. In summer the weather is almost always good, but with hot and damp spells that call for a quick refreshing dip in the sea. In the transition periods of May, September and October you may come across rainy days and storms. In winter, although on sunny days you can enjoy fairly high above-average temperatures (the minimum is 7°C (45°F), the maximum 17°C) (63°F), the wind whips through the narrow streets of the towns. Sometimes the snow reaches the coast, creating an unusual and captivating spectacle. Especially at the end of summer the coast is often swept by strong southwest winds that raise spectacular heavy seas.

October 25, 2011: Muddy Hell

It was October 25, 2011 when in less than six hours more than 400 mm (almost sixteen inches) of rain fell on Vernazza and Monterosso. Tons of mud and rocks fell from the hills, the streams swelled and the streets of the two towns turned into overflowing rivers of mud, which in some cases reached the second floors of the houses, destroying everything in their path. Houses, shops, bars, hotels and restaurants were swept away in just a few minutes. Cars sank into the sea. The marinas and squares crumbled under the fury of the water and four people found their deaths there.

It is thanks to the thousands of volunteers who arrived from all over the world that the towns have come to life again and found the strength to react to the catastrophe. In just a few months the so-called "mud angels", with their shovels and boots freed the wounded towns and the people could move back into their homes. Day after day life in the Cinque Terre returned to what it was before the flood.

Walking through the streets of Vernazza, which today has recovered its ancient beauty, you will come across doors with paintings: this is a gift to the town by the "artist angels" from La Spezia. In the church at Monterosso the signs of the mud on the walls have been preserved and a plaque on the outside recalls the level reached by the flood that had submerged the town in 1966 as well.

Flora

In the Cinque Terre you can find some fairly rare plant species which are under the protection of the park authorities.

In spring, large yellow bushes color the coast. These are exemplars of **euforbia arborea**, a species characterized by small yellow spring flowers. In summer the plant sheds its leaves and seems to be dry and dead, but this is its strategy to survive the heat of a scorching sun.

Following the discovery of America, many South American species have appeared since they found a suitable climate here. So the **prickly pear** has now colonized the coasts, together with the **agave**, with its large, hooking leaves. Sometimes a stem rises from the center of this plant: it is its flower which blooms only when the plant has reached maturity and just before its death. Naturally, the presence of vineyards, olive and citrus groves are characteristic of the hills behind the towns, but higher up there are stands of **pine** and **chestnut**, which were once the staples of the inhabitants.

Many Mediterranean bushes and shrubs grow on the rocks, such as **Spanish broom**, **myrtle** and plants with small colored flowers known as "**erba cristallina**" (ice plant), that grow on the cliffs.

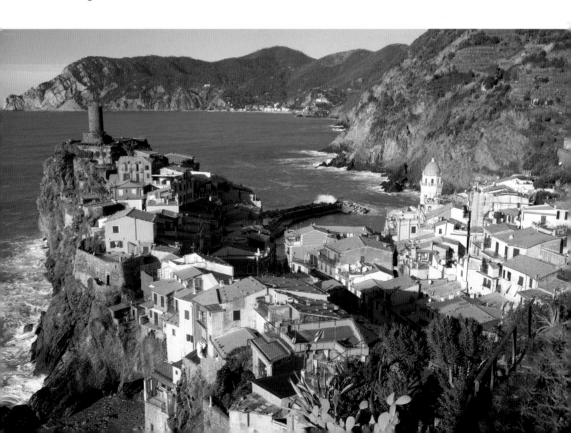

Riomaggiore

Reliable mentions of the town's existence date from the 13th century. The name derives from the stream that flows through the valley, the *Rivus Maior* (biggest river) which today flows under the main street (Via Colombo), but up to the early 20th century it was in view. The houses were connected by bridges and for this reason the

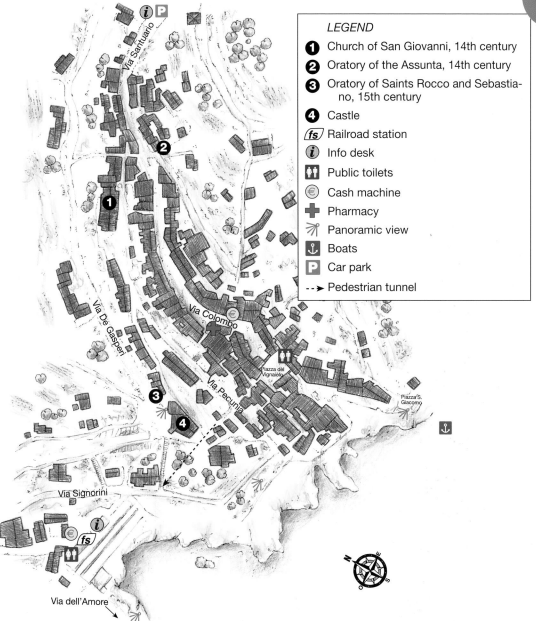

LEGEND

1. Church of San Giovanni, 14th century
2. Oratory of the Assunta, 14th century
3. Oratory of Saints Rocco and Sebastiano, 15th century
4. Castle

fs Railroad station

i Info desk

Public toilets

€ Cash machine

Pharmacy

Panoramic view

Boats

P Car park

--► Pedestrian tunnel

town was known as "Little Venice". How Riomaggiore was in those times can be seen in the paintings by **Telemaco Signorini**, a famous Italian artist who lived at the end of the 19th century and who was fascinated by the landscape.

The marvels of the place come to the fore a little at a time on walking up Via Colombo or taking the panoramic Via Signorini which starts from the square in front of the station. There is a train tunnel just after the park offices near the station that takes you to the heart of the town in a few min-utes. In the tunnel, 157 meters (515 feet) in length, there is a mosaic by the artist **Silvio Benedetto**, whose preference is representing human labor. He is also the artist who painted the large picture in the station and the *murales* on the façade of the town hall and elementary school.

A **castle** overlooks the town: it was built in its defense in 1260 by the Turcotti family, the lords of the town. It was part of a larger system of defense of which little remains today. Up to about twenty years ago the building was used as a cemetery.

Following restoration, it now belongs to the park and is used for meetings and ceremonies.

In front of the castle is the small **oratory of Saints Rocco and Sebastiano** (end of the 15th century) built after a plague to offer thanks for surviving the danger.

The church (1340) is named for **St. John the Baptist**. Of the original structure there remains the right hand wall, the one facing the square, decorated with the heads of monstrous animals, typical of the Gothic style. The façade is the result of restoration in the 19th century. Inside are many chapels and works of art by local artists, among which the *Predicazione del Battista*,

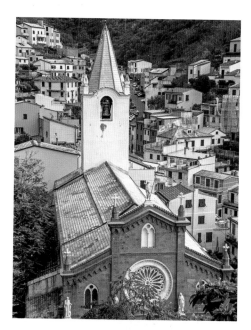

attributed to Domenico Fiasella (1589 - 1669).

Another oratory is dedicated to **Santa Maria Assunta** in the area known as *la compagnia*, (the company) a place where the town elderly gather to enjoy the hours of the siesta.

A visit to the **marina**, the small port for fishing and pleasure craft, is a must. The many colors of the fishing boats, the nets spread out to dry and the typical houses painted in lively colors make this one of the most fascinating places in the town. From here, climbing the stairway on the left, you can arrive at the landing stage and the public beach known as the *Fossola*, with large pebbles. Riomaggiore's sea conceals a mysterious seabed rich in protected species where you can also come across sunken ships which make it perfect for **diving** and **snorkeling.**

For those who prefer shopping or wish to enjoy good ice cream, the best place to start is Via Colombo, where the old dwellings of the farmers have now become shops offering typical products and souvenirs.

Riomaggiore dresses up for Corpus Domini and Pentecost, when there is the feast of the **Madonna di Monte Nero**, whose ancient sanctuary (1335 c.), to which the faithful attribute many miraculous events, can be seen on the Monte Nero hill overlooking the town.

Via dell'Amore

This "trail of love" is an easy-to-walk romantic path about one kilometer (3280 feet) long that connects Riomaggiore to Manarola. This path, like the others in the Cinque Terre, may be closed or not open the entire distance, so it is best to enquire at park offices or consult the website www.parconazionale5terre.it before starting out. It was laid out starting from the 1920s when work began to improve the railroad line that tunnels through the mountain. The inhabitants of the two towns worked hard on building the trail; they were volunteer workers who received no pay for

putting their lives at risk. In fact, as many as three men died while working there. Before its inauguration, Manarola and Riomaggiore were connected only by the trail that winds through the vineyards. It was not an easy one to follow since it meant going over the top of the hill after climbing up a steep stairway. So the shorter and most heavily travelled route, the "new road", which owes the name *Via dell'Amore* to the Italian journalist **Paolo Monelli** who was inspired by the fact that during the Second World War the young people of the two towns met here in a romantic setting, perfect for lovers.

Unique of its kind, there is also a botanic oasis where many protected species grow. The coast is steep and rugged and the trail was literally excavated by man. Landslides and rock falls are frequent and the trail has to be closed when there are storms at sea and weather alarms. The Via dell'Amore is also completely accessible to the disabled. Along the way there are places for resting and a few paths down to the sea.

In the most romantic places in the Cinque Terre, and especially along the Via dell'Amore, you will find hundreds of padlocks attached to the walls or wedged into the rocks. This is a recent fashion and is the symbol of eternal love. Padlocks are on sale in shops selling souvenirs.

Manarola

The town, with a layout similar to that of Riomaggiore, was built on the banks of a stream, the Rio Groppo, which still flows under the main streets (Via Discovolo and Via Birolli). The origin of the name is not certain; some believe it derives from the Latin *magna Roea* meaning the large wheel. In support of this, halfway through the town there is still a large ancient waterwheel which is thought to have given the name, but this is only a theory.

Manarola's inhabitants once lived in the ancient hamlet of **Volastra**, which rises on the hill. They came down to the valley following a plague epidemic and founded one of the Cinque Terre. Its existence is documented starting from the 14th century.

From the station you go through a tunnel, 180 meters (590 feet) in length, on the

LEGEND
1 Church of San Lorenzo, 14th c.
2 Oratory
3 Bell tower, ancient tower
4 Ancient mill
5 Bastion, 16th century
6 Remains of fortifications
fs Railroad station
i Info desk
Public toilets
€ Cash machine
Pharmacy
Panoramic view
Boats
Pedestrian tunnel

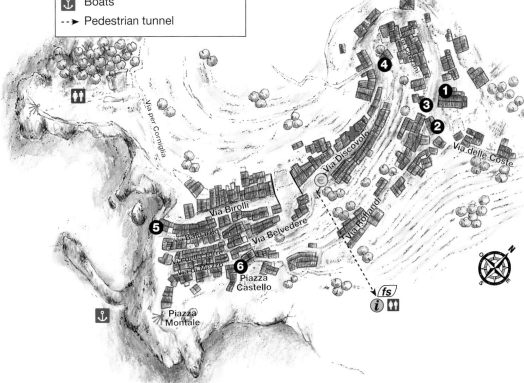

walls of which are images of the Cinque Terre National Park. On arriving in Via Discovolo, you turn left to reach the sea, the **marina** and the landing slip.

If you turn right in the direction of the hill, you can walk up and discover the treasures in the town's main church.

For those who reach the town with their own means of transportation, from the parking lot we suggest going down to the sea the easy way, following the main street, crossing the typical *carruggi*, the narrow streets leading to the sea, or taking the paths through the vineyards. Finding the direction is easy: all you need to know is that all streets lead to the sea!

There is one path to mention in particular: it is easy and panoramic and starts from behind the church. It is the so-called *manarolino* which goes through the fields and terraces and takes you to the sea in about fifteen minutes.

The town's most important church is **San Lorenzo** which overlooks the houses. Built

in the Gothic style in 1338 using local sandstone, it presents a magnificent rose window with white Carrara marble with human and lion heads on the outer crown. Inside are the works of the **Maestro delle Cinque Terre**, an artist who lived at the end of the 15th century and who painted two of the church's tryptics; one is in the left nave and portrays Saint Lawrence at the center

together with Saints Bernard and Anthony. On observing carefully, you can see a gridiron at the saint's feet: according to the religious tradition Lawrence was burned to death on a gridiron. Behind the Baroque high altar is another work by the Maestro depicting the Madonna and Child and the saints Lawrence and Catherine, who can be recognized by the presence of the spiked wheel, the symbol of her martyrdom. In front of the façade you find the **bell tower**, which was once a watchtower. Still in the square, you see the **Oratory of the Disciplinati**, once an ancient hospital and today used for exhibitions. Going down towards the sea, along the street you come to the mill mentioned before and which perhaps gave the name to the town. Just after the tunnel that goes to the station there is a square dedicated to Dario Capellini, an antifascist partisan who later became a provincial administrator. Here you can admire the fine mosaic pavement decorated with ceramic sea gulls and fishes. The train runs under the square, so if you feel the pavement shake, don't be afraid! Continuing on you come to the sea. From the marina there is a complete view of the small inlet for boats which was excavated in the rock. Today, the fishermen put their boats in the water using a *paranco*, similar to a tackle, which you can see from the square. After visiting the port, we suggest going on along the promenade to **Punta Buonfiglio**, about a ten-minute walk. If instead you are looking for the landing slip you have to go down the stairs on the left of the square.

There is a magnificent view of the town from the Punta Buonfiglio promontory. Also visible are Corniglia and Monterosso, while Vernazza is hidden behind the

promontory. There are some sculptures in the park which are the works of contemporary artists. One of these is an allegory of the grape harvest.

Manarola does not lose its fascination when the sun goes down. On the 10th of August of every year the night of San Lorenzo, "the night of the falling stars" is celebrated with a procession led by the statue of the saint which goes from the church down to the sea. At Christmas time you can see the renowned illuminated Nativity scene, a work of extraordinary evocative power created by **Mario Andreoli**, a former railroad man, who covers the hillside every year with scenes from the birth of Jesus, all done with discarded material: a true work of art!

Corniglia

Among the theories on the origin of the name, there is the evocative one that it is of Roman origin. In reality there is no evidence that the coast was inhabited at the time of the Romans, but we do have proof of the existence of Corniglia in the Middle Ages, when the town was known at the courts of European monarchs owing to the excellent wine produced here.

The town's elevated position, defended by the rugged terrain as well as by defensive works put in place by the inhabitants, made it one of the lookout posts against pirate raids in the Cinque Terre in the past.

Corniglia is the only one of the Cinque Terre that is not directly on the coast; it can be reached on foot by climbing up an easy brick stairway called the **Lardarina**. It has thirty-three ramps and a total of 377 steps, fortunately not overly steep. There is a convenient shuttle bus that can take you to the town from the railroad station.

Corniglia is on a rocky promontory with cliffs down to the sea, about a hundred meters (328 feet) below. From the town you can enjoy a breathtaking panorama, one that is unique of its kind. The town lies along the main street, Via Fieschi, a *carruggio* where you can still smell the odors of the wine cellars, especially at the time of the harvest.

The town can be divided into two. From the bus stop on the square, turning right

LEGEND

❶ Church of San Pietro, 13th century
❷ Medieval buildings
❸ Oratory, 17th century
❹ Remains of fortifications
fs Railroad station
ⓘ Info desk
🚻 Public toilets
€ Cash machine
🏹 Panoramic view
📇 Stairway to the sea

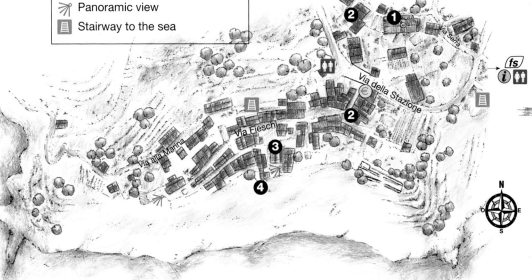

and going up a few stairs, you come to the main church, **San Pietro** (1334). It was built thanks to money raised by the town's inhabitants. Inside are works of art from the 15th to the 19th century, mostly by local artists. In the lunette of the façade is a small statue representing St. Peter with the keys in his hand: in the Christian tradition he is in fact the guardian of Heaven. If you look closely you will see a deer, an emblem of Christ and an allegory of the Resurrection.

Near the church is one of the town's oldest **case torri** (tower houses) where there are some bas reliefs sculpted on the door posts. According to historians, this was the old post office of the Fieschi family, an important Genoese family whose dominions also included the Cinque Terre.

Still from the bus station parking lot, if you turn left and take the *carruggio*, you will come to the historic center of the town. In a few minutes you are in the **Largo Teragio**, a small square cool in the shade of the plane trees. At the center is a bronze sculpture dedicated to those who died in the Second World War. Behind the statue is a small church dedicated to **Santa Caterina**: it is the oratory of the *Disciplinati*, the seat of the town's brotherhood. If you go up the stairs you come to a first terrace called the *Fossa*, where you can see Manarola clinging to the coast as well as the entire beach of Corniglia. Here you can see the fragility of the land: the signs of the large

landslides that often block the path to Manarola can be seen with the naked eye.

Those who wish to climb the steep stairs on the right (not many steps) can enjoy the same view from higher up. The walls supporting the second terrace are, according to some historians, the remains of the curtain wall of an ancient castle or watchtower.

Continuing the visit to the town, you go along the *carruggio* that leads to another terrace offering a sweeping view of the crystalline sea from the top of a cliff. From here, you can see on the right the Punta Mesco cape, the outermost boundary of the Cinque Terre; the town you see on the coast is Monterosso. Moving closer, there is a partial view of Vernazza. Shifting your glance up the hill you cannot miss the bell tower of the hamlet of **San Bernardino**, with the church of the same name clinging to the rock. You will also see the farmers' gardens with the never-lacking vineyards but also citrus trees, mostly oranges. On the right you can clearly see Manarola, a part of Riomaggiore and, finally the cape of Montenero.

Vernazza

With Monterosso, Vernazza is the oldest town of the Cinque Terre; the first mentions of it date back to 1080 and confirm that even then it was important. Walking through its streets you can still see the remains of this memorable medieval past. It also played an important role in the history of the Republic of Genoa, which stationed some of the galeae of its fleet in roads here.

Vernazza was also built along a stream, the Vernaz-zola, which emptied into the sea. The name, leaving aside certain imaginative hypotheses of a Roman origin, appears to derive from *verna*, which means "indigenous" or "local" and thus is thought to have the same etymology as the *Vernaccia* wine.

Going down the stairs of the station you will see on your left a panel with pictures of the disastrous flood which devastated the town on October 25, 2011. On the walls you can still see signs of the destructive force of the mud, which reached the second floors of the houses.

Going through the underpass you come to the small Piazzetta dei Caduti, restored after the 2011 flood. In the center is a large millstone recalling the agricultural vocation of the town, which is one of the most famed

LEGEND

1 Church of Santa Margherita, 14th century
2 Belforte bastion
3 Castle and tower, 13th century
4 Medieval buildings
5 San Francesco, church and convent, 17th c.
6 Medieval arches
7 Ancient mill
fs Railroad station
i Info desk
Public toilets
€ Cash machine
+ Pharmacy
Boats
Panoramic view

producers of olive oil but most of all of wine, such as *Vernaccia*, which has been appreciated since the Middle Ages. Along the main street, Via Roma, you cannot miss seeing the typical medieval **ogival arches** made with local green stone. On the left of the street is the small chapel of **Santa Marta**, once again bearing witness to popular devotion. Just past there, the street branches off to the left where there is the grotto "of the Devil". Before the flood the sea arrived here, but the torrent of detritus that was washed down from the mountain found a natural outlet here and created a new beach beyond it in a few hours.

The **marina** is at the end of the street where there is one of eastern Liguria's most picturesque views. Piazza Marconi is where the town's fishermen and visitors gather. The people of Vernazza are accustomed to spending the *siesta* hours under the arches of the building.

On the left is a stairway that leads up to the **castle** (124 steps). Originally the town was fortified, but today of the ancient walls,

which continued down to the sea, only a few parts near the cemetery remain, together with what is left of the castle. From here you can buy a ticket to climb to the top of the tower, which offers a magnificent panorama. The round **tower**, the same from which the sentinels kept watch against attacks from the sea, dates back to the 13th century. It was part of a complex and effective system of defense of the town and from the top you can see the entire town: the church of Santa Margherita by the sea, the **Church and Convent of San Francesco** (17th century) on the hill. In its courtyard there is an ancient defense tower from which start the remains of the crenellated **curtain wall** and the cemetery. The hills are terraced with vineyards and olive groves. Looking towards Corniglia you will see another round tower which some years ago was found to be an ancient windmill with vanes originally inside. On the horizon

is Monterosso with its beaches and the Punta del Mesco.

From Piazza Marconi you can visit the main church, **Santa Margherita di Antiochia**, nicknamed the *sauroctona*, which means "dragon killer". The church was built in 1318 in the Ligurian Gothic style using serpentinite, a local green stone. The entrance is now in the back of the church: the semicircular structure of the apse can be seen clearly. In the past, access to the church was through the side facing the mountains but it was modified between the 16th and 17th centuries. At the beginning of the 20th century, the Baroque ornamentation was removed, thus restoring the building to its original aspect in stone and the wooden roof was restored. So today the atmosphere is rather austere but quite

fascinating and from the windows there is a splendid view of the marina.

Vernazza's **marina** is dedicated to "the people of the sea". In the square decorated with mosaics people wait for the arrival of the passenger boats and it is possible to rent kayaks and private boats. Although it is quite a picturesque place, it is best not to get too close to take pictures when the sea is rough: the waves break violently against the jetty.

Above the marina is a bastion, the Belforte. From here, facing the town you will have a magnificent view of the *case torri* (tower houses), so-called owing to their height. They were built side against side for defensive reasons.

Monterosso

LEGEND

1. Oratory of the Bianchi, 17th century
2. Medieval portico
3. Medieval palace
4. Oratory of the Neri, 17th century
5. Church of San Giovanni, 13th c.
6. San Francesco, church and convent, 17th century
7. Aurora tower
8. Remains of medieval fortifications

fs Railroad station
ⓘ Info desk
🚻 Public toilets
ⓔ Cash machine
✚ Pharmacy
⚓ Boats
✈ Panoramic view
⤍ Pedestrian tunnel

even then the town was quite important. The original nucleus of Monterosso, like that of the other towns, rose on the banks of a stream, the Rio Buranco, which today flows under Via Roma, the main street.

Today the town is divided into two nuclei. The separation is visible whether you arrive by sea, train or by private transportation.

The "new" part is that of **Fegina**, where there are the beaches and many hotels. The town became a tourist attraction following the opening of the station, which is at Fegina. From this side of the town an en-

Together with Vernazza, it is the oldest town of the Cinque Terre, but it is also the largest and most capacious for visits and accommodations. Evidence of its existence goes back to 1056, when an important document, *in loco Monte Russo,* was signed to prove that

joyable promenade leads to the area of the *gigante* (the giant), which is beyond the sports field and the car park. This is a huge statue fourteen meters (46 feet) in height at the foot of the mountain representing Neptune, the god of the sea of the ancients. The imposing figure was sculpted partly in the rock and partly with reinforced concrete by Arrigo Minerbi in 1910. At one time the statue supported on its shoulders the terrace of the Villa Pastine in the form of a seashell, which today has been lost after being damaged by bombs during the Second World War (1939-1945). Still in this area, for those fond of *Art Nouveau* architecture there is the Ville Montale, a residential complex that belonged to **Eugenio Montale**, the Italian poet and Nobel laureate, who spent his holidays here and found inspiration for his works.

For those who arrive from the station, Monterosso's old town center can be reached by turning left and going through the tunnel. Or from near the tunnel you can turn right and take a short walk that follows the coast of **Capo San Cristoforo**. The original nucleus of Monterosso was at the top of the hill, around the no longer extant San Cristoforo castrum church which gives its name to the hill. Here you can see the remains of the ancient *castrum* and the **citadel** is still visible with machicolations and embrasures on the walls with Ghibelline battlements. You can reach the top of the hill by taking the stairway leading to the **convent of the Capuchin friars** and the **church of San Francesco** (17th century) of whom there is a bronze statue by Silvio Monfrini halfway up, where you can enjoy a splendid panorama. Inside the

church are many works of art, among which a Crucifixion which tradition considers the work of the Flemish painter Van Dyck, (1599-1641), but this attribution has been contradicted by recent studies.

The "old" town has the church at its center and overlooks a small beach. Once beyond the arches of the elevated railroad, you come to Piazza Garibaldi, which has been restored following the 2011 flood. The portico is the back of the main church, **San Giovanni Battista,** which dates from the 13th century. The façade is one of the most beautiful in the area with its two colors (white marble and serpentine) which is typical of churches built in the Ligurian Gothic style. The magnificent rose window is composed of eighteen small columns as its radii.

On entering, the bichrome pillars, the ancient baptismal font and the Baroque altar of polychrome marble come into view.

In the square in front of the church another religious edifice makes a fine show of itself. It is the oratory of the so-called **Neri** brotherhood. Built in the 17th century thanks to donations by the people of Monterosso, on the façade is the Latin inscription *mortis et orationis* (death and prayer). The brotherhood that administered the oratory was dedicated to prayer and helping the needy and those who could not afford a proper burial. The lugubrious but noble duty of the brothers is seen inside the building, decorated with stuccoes representing skulls and allegories of Death. The unsettling furniture of the wooden chorus is truly quite realistic. These are *memento mori*, that is, metaphors and alle-

gories reminding visitors and the faithful that all must die.

In the small square in front of the church there is also a **building** with a portico of typical Ligurian form which presents medieval arches in black stone and frames with small blind arches on the outside wall to the south. The building probably dates back to the 13th century and originally stood alone with a portico, but today it is part of later construction work.

In Monterosso you can visit another oratory, that of Santa Croce, known as the oratory of the **Bianchi**, owing to the white tunics worn by the brothers.

The ancient **Torre Aurora**, on a cliff overlooking the sea, was once a lookout post and defensive outpost.

So as not to miss the liveliness of the town, you can stroll through its narrow and fascinating vaulted *carruggi,* maybe sipping a good glass of local wine.

The Railroad

The railroad that passes through the Cinque Terre is the one that connects La Spezia to Genoa and is one of Italy's oldest, built in the years from 1860 to 1874 with a layout quite close to the sea. Later, in the 20th century, the line was changed by laying the tracks farther inland, adding another track and building wider tunnels. You will see that this is a gigantic work of engineering and architecture even if you visit the Cinque Terre by sea. At the Manarola and Corniglia stations it was in fact necessary to place huge retaining walls.

The stations are all rather small, with the exception of those of Corniglia and Monterosso. At the Vernazza station the train

is often forced to stop in the tunnel, thus making it difficult for passengers to get on and off. There is a ticket counter as well as shops and park offices at every station. The public toilets are also near the station. Once you have entered the town you can also use the rest rooms in the bars and restaurants if need be, but in such cases it is best to order something.

The boats

Although the train is undoubtedly the quickest and cheapest way to reach the Cinque Terre, there is nothing that compares to the sight you can enjoy on arriving by sea. The Consorzio Marittimo Turistico Cinque Terre-Golfo dei Poeti offers boat connections which operate from the end of March to the beginning of November. Except for Corniglia, where there is no port, all the towns are connected by boats on the hour; at Portovenere there are connections to La Spezia and Lerici by lines that vary seasonally. You can tour the three islands of Palmaria, Tino and Tinetto only from Portovenere. Even Levanto can be reached by sea: the connection to Monterosso is guaranteed by two daily runs.

Trips are cancelled when the sea is rough and weather conditions are prohibitive. If it is rough but still navigable, only the direct routes from Portovenere to Monterosso are open, but with no calls at the other four towns.

The beaches

Considering the lay of the land, there are not many sandy beaches in the area, but some of these are equipped with all comforts. At Monterosso, the Fegina beaches and those of the ancient hamlet are partly free and partly paid. For an umbrella, beach chair or chaise longue you have to buy a ticket to enter the beach.

As we have seen, at Vernazza the fury of the flood waters was so great that it created a new beach beside the old one near the marina. To reach this lovely beach you have to pass through the small tunnel along the main street.

Corniglia also had a beach near the station, but today it has been almost completely washed away by the sea. Quite fa-

mous in the 1970s was Corniglia's picturesque **Guvano** beach, which was the site of a hippy colony and still today is a beach for naturists. It can be reached by going through the old tunnel.

There are no beaches at Manarola, but access to the sea is provided by two inlets. One is at the marina and the other is sheltered by Punta Buonfiglio. It is called **Palaedo** and is renowned for its incredibly clear water. There are also many rocky inlets and shoals along the Via dell'Amore but be careful, to go bathing here you have to be good swimmers and not afraid of the depths because the sea is deep just off the coast and you have to dive into the blue with no hesitation! It is best not to bathe

when the sea is getting rough since it can be extremely dangerous: the backwash of the waves is quite strong.

Riomaggiore has a stony beach with large pebbles that are rather slippery. Instead, at Portovenere the water is calmer and you can find beaches along the coast. But if you want to swim in the open sea or discover small caves and views of the still uncontaminated coast, you can rent a canoe, kayak or pleasure boat in all the towns.

La Spezia and
the Gulf of the Poets

La Spezia, the second most important town in Liguria, is at the center of a magnificent gulf, one of Italy's most tranquil and best protected anchorages. For this reason it was chosen by Napoleon Bonaparte (Emperor of France, King of Italy from 1805 to 1814) as the base for his fleet. He had great plans for the city and gulf and he began by building a system of defense and designing an **arsenal**. That plan was never implemented and only in 1869, thanks to Cavour (prime minister of the Kingdom of Italy) and General Domenico Chiodo, was a large arsenal built.

Although La Spezia and its gulf were frequented already at the time of the Romans and in its old center you can see traces of past centuries, such as the **Castello San Giorgio**, the town walls, the medieval portals and 17th-century palaces, the city expanded most starting from the second half of the 19th century. In those years La Spezia grew and became one of the capitals of the *Liberty* style, which in Italy corresponds to **Art Nouveau**. Also not to be missed is a visit to the historic stairways such as the **Scalinata della Cernaia** or to the 19th century **public gardens** extending over 80,000 square meters (864,000 sq. ft.) and with elegant antique furnishings which are still fascinating, even though today they are a bit neglected. There is also a wide variety of plants representing over 170 species. In the town's museums you

can enjoy works of art of all epochs, from the Roman collections on display at the Castello San Giorgio, to the exhibitions at the Naval Museum, the refined works of the greatest Italian artists in the Lia Collection and the futurist colors and challenges of contemporary art promoted by the Camec, La Spezia's museum of modern and contemporary art.

For all these reasons, La Spezia is an excellent place to visit. It is easily reached by train and private car, but also by boat (for brevity's sake the city's attractions are not described at length here. For more in-depth information you will find many publications available or "Tourist Map – central points of historic and artistic interest" in the kiosks and souvenir shops).

The Gulf of the Poets and the archipelago

The gulf measures 4.5 km (2.8 miles) in length and approximately 3.5 km (2 miles) in breadth. A breakwater about 2210 meters (7250 feet) long protects the harbor from the waves and ships can enter through two passages. You will see these clearly if you reach Portovenere or the Cinque Terre by boat. Quite picturesque hamlets appear on the shores of the gulf. Among those on the western shores we can mention **Fezzano, Cadimare** and **Le Grazie**, where you can visit the archaeological site of a **Roman villa** bearing witness to the presence of the ancient Romans in the gulf. The eastern shore is instead a long series of shipyards which have made La Spezia one of the leading cities in this sector. You then come to **San Terenzo, Lerici** and **Tellaro**, quite romantic places rich in history and loved by poets such as Shelley, Byron, George Sand, D.H. Lawrence and many other artists and painters who found a source of inspiration in the gulf. For this reason it is known as the Gulf of the Poets.

Three islands crown this part of the sea: **Palmaria**, **Tino** and **Tinetto**, which form La Spezia's archipelago. These, together with Portovenere and the Cinque Terre, were declared a UNESCO World Heritage Site in 1997. With its wealth of exceptional historic, botanic and wildlife attractions, since 2001 this area has been a part of the Regional Park whose duty is to conserve its beauty.

The island of Palmaria is the largest (1.89 km^2) (0.73 sq. miles) with many trails and unique views. You can also visit the 19th-century fortifications and those of the Second World War. The islet of Tino (0.13 km^2) (0.05 sq. mi) belongs to the Italian Navy so you cannot land on it either by private craft or scheduled lines, but it can be admired from the sea. Here lived the hermit San Venerio (who died in 630), the patron saint of the gulf, who is celebrated on September 13th of each year. At the time of his feast you can land and visit the remains of the ancient monastery (11th to the 14th centuries). The third islet, Tinetto, is nothing more than a shoal, but nonetheless even here you can find the ruins of a medieval religious settlement.

Portovenere

From the ancient Roman settlements in the area, borne witness to by numerous findings, the name of Portovenere (*Portus Veneris*), undoubtedly comes from Venus, the goddess of beauty. Portovenere is an ancient medieval town of seafaring folk which still today conserves its ancient structure as well as many signs of its origin. It is at the western end of the gulf and rises in a strategic position. Facing the sea, it was the perfect site for controlling maritime traffic. For this reason it was disputed by the Republics of Genoa and Pisa. In 1113 it was sold by the lords of Vezzano and became Genoese. Many battles were fought to conquer the town: the bloodiest

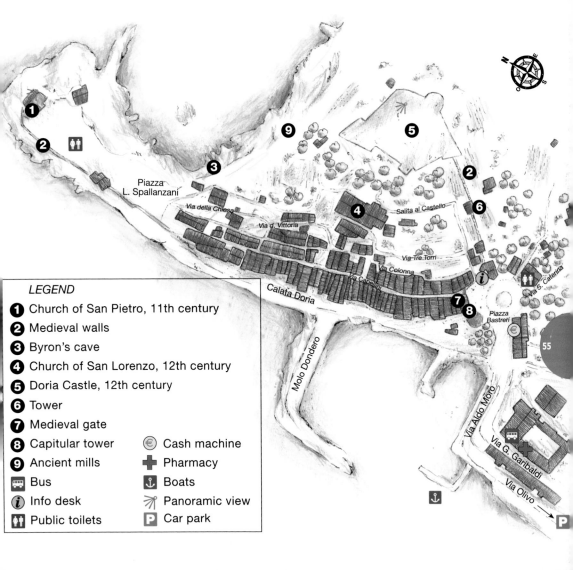

LEGEND

❶ Church of San Pietro, 11th century
❷ Medieval walls
❸ Byron's cave
❹ Church of San Lorenzo, 12th century
❺ Doria Castle, 12th century
❻ Tower
❼ Medieval gate
❽ Capitular tower
❾ Ancient mills
🚌 Bus
ⓘ Info desk
🚻 Public toilets

€ Cash machine
✚ Pharmacy
⚓ Boats
🗺 Panoramic view
🅿 Car park

was in 1494, when it was razed to the ground by the troops of Charles VIII, King of France.

Although the town is now part of the province of La Spezia, the Genoese flags still wave on its towers, the symbol of a lasting bond.

The church of **San Pietro** (11th century) at the end of the Arpaia promontory was probably erected on the ruins of a Roman building. The church today is the result of 19th-century restoration, but traces of a past rich in history are still visible. The façade, with its alternation of white Carrara marble and black marble called *Portoro*, is typical of Ligurian architecture in the Gothic period. You can climb up to the roof and take charming photos from the loggia overlooking the sea.

The area below San Pietro still shows the remains of the ancient system of defense.

Before reaching the church, at the bottom of the stairway is a path to the sea where you will see a cavity in the rock. This is the cave dedicated to **Lord Byron** (1788-1824), the English poet and politician who often sojourned at San Terenzo (another hamlet on the coast of the gulf) at the villa of his friend Shelley. According to a legend, every summer the poet swam from San Terenzo to Portovenere, crossing the entire gulf and challenging the waves. From this panoramic point you will also see the hamlet's fascinating **cemetery** and the huge **castle**, the stronghold of the complex system of defense that made Portovenere an invincible fortress. The central part of the castle dates back to the 12th century, but it later underwent many changes and additions. Visits to the castle are not free of charge. You can reach it by going up the wide stairway that starts in the square, leaving behind you the church of San Pietro.

In several places you can still see parts of the **curtain walls,** such as those con-

necting the castle to the ancient **town gate**, on which there is a stone with the date on which Portovenere became Genoese (1113). Among the most significant monuments is the **capitulary tower**, which stands out on the left of the entrance to the town. Everything in Portovenere's layout indicates its origin in the Middle Ages.

Along the way to the castle is another ancient church, **San Lorenzo** (12th century). Inside are many works of art, among which the *Madonna Bianca*. The image represents the *Virgin with Child* which according to the legend arrived at Portovenere inside a tree trunk which still today is kept in the left nave. It is said that the miraculous image saved the townsfolk from a plague on August 17, 1399. At the time of the feast of the Madonna Bianca, which is on August 17th, the place fills with lights and candles are lit on the rocks down to the sea, creating a night scene of great effect.

You cannot leave without a stroll along the promenade to admire the so-called *palazzata* with the typical "tower houses" in a tight row to defend the place against sieges: today they present a fascinating view alive with color.

Inside, in the *carruggio*, with its many workshops and souvenir shops, you can admire the remains of the remote past such as the beautiful sculpted medieval portals. The two ramps, rather steep but quite fascinating, which take you from the *carruggio* to the sea, are called the **capitoli**.

References

Roberta Ferraris (cur.), *Cinque Terre e Golfo dei Poeti*, Touring Editore/Slow food editore Milano, 2013.

Diego Savani (cur.), *La Spezia - carta turistica. Guida storico-artistica del centro città*, Edizioni Giacché La Spezia, 2013.

Diego Savani (cur.), *La Spezia Tourist Map - Central points of historic and artistic interest*, Edizioni Giacché La Spezia, 2013.

Mauro Mariotti (cur.), *Cinque Terre-Portovenere-Isola Palmaria*, Ligurpress Genova, 2012.

Albano Marcarini, *I sentieri delle Cinque Terre*, Lyasis Sondrio, 2008.

Alberto Girani, *Guida alle Cinque Terre*, Sagep Genova, 2007.

Attilio Casavecchia-Enrica Salvatori, *La storia e la pietra*, Parco Nazionale delle Cinque Terre, 2003.

Paola Gaione, *Via dell'Amore. Viaggio nelle Cinque Terre*, Edizioni Giacché La Spezia, 1995.

Paolo Emilio Faggioni, *Vini e Vigneti delle Cinque Terre*, Stringa Genova, 1983.

Clario di Fabio, *L'architettura ecclesiastica a Portovenere fra XI e XIV secolo*, in *San Venerio del Tino: vita religiosa e terraferma in età medievale*, Atti del Convegno 18-20 settembre 1982, Istituto Internazionale di Studi Liguri-sezione Lunense, La Spezia, 1986.

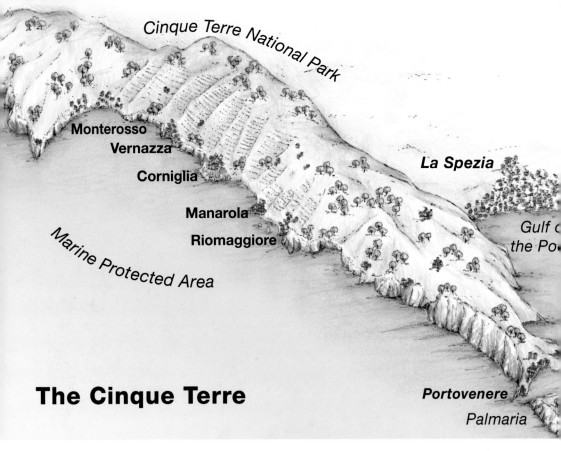

Cinque Terre National Park

Monterosso
Vernazza
Corniglia

La Spezia

Manarola
Riomaggiore

Marine Protected Area

Gulf of
the Po...

The Cinque Terre

Portovenere
Palmaria

Texts: Diego Savani
Graphics: Irene Giacché
English translation: David C. Nilson
Maps: Pamela Preti and Irene Giacché for © Edizioni Giacché

Photographs: ©Edizioni Giacché: pag. 7 Nello Biondi; 8 Irene Giacché; 9a Walter Meloni; 9b Irene Giacché;
10 Walter Meloni; 14-15 Walter Meloni; 16a Cristian Polloni; 19 Nello Biondi; 20 Daniele Giannetti;
23a Carmelo Di Fiore; 25 Cristian Polloni; 29a Walter Meloni; 29b Cristian Polloni; 30a Franco Guelfi;
34b Irene Giacché; 35 Daniele Giannetti; 37 Cristian Polloni; 40 e 45 Carmelo di Fiore; 49 Daniele Giannetti;
51-52 Daniele Giannetti; 57 Fabio Mercugliano; 61 Daniele Giannetti; back cover Daniele Giannetti.

Photographs: ©Agenzia Thinkstock/iStock: front cover Jenifoto; pag. 1 Emicristea; 2-3 Mihtiander; 4 Massimo Vaccari;
6 Anton Jackson; 11 123455543; 12 Gio-tto; 16b Emicristea; 17 Anshar73; 18 Medioimages/Photodisc;
22 Frank Fischbach; 23b Porojnicu; 24 Johnny 007Pan; 26 Hors; 28 Sebastien Burel; 30b Eurotravel; 31 Anshar73;
32 123455543; 34a Emicristea; 36 Krasnevsy; 38 Simone Kesh; 41 Roman Rodionov; 42 Stevan Zz; 43 Freeartist;
44 Frank Fischbach; 45 Ahavelaar; 47 Krasnevsy; 48 MartinM303; 50 Ueua Photo; 53 Vora; 54 Ueua Photo; 56 Topdeq;
58 Viti; 59 Anton Jackson; 60 Jenifoto; 62-63 Top Photo Corporation.

This book is printed on forest-friendly FSC paper.
The FSC logo indicates products containing paper from
forests managed in accordance with the strict environmental,
economic and social standards defined by the Forest
Stewardship Council.

Edizioni Giacché loves solar energy.
Company powered by photovoltaic panels

www.edizionigiacche.com

© Edizioni Giacché - 3rd print May 2016 (1st print March 2014). Printed by Geca Srl - MI

"Great Travelers" Series

Large format photo books which reconstruct historical itineraries of illustrious travelers of the past. Full page photographs.
Hardback, full color, by Shelley, Byron, Virginia Woolf, D.H. Lawrence, Henry James, George Sand and others. Italian, English, French, and German texts

LA SPEZIA. TOURIST MAP

Central points of historic and artistic interest

Italian, English, Spanish and French version

The most beautiful buildings in theold centre of town:
the Castle, the medieval portals, the 17th-century mansions.

The buildings in the Art Nouveau, Art Decò and Futurist styles.
The monuments, museums, squares, streets and historical stairways.

Details of the centre of town.
Scale: 1:3000

TOURIST GUIDE series

www.edizionigiacche.com

FSC
www.fsc.org

MIX
Paper from
responsible sources
FSC® C007287

9 788863 820522